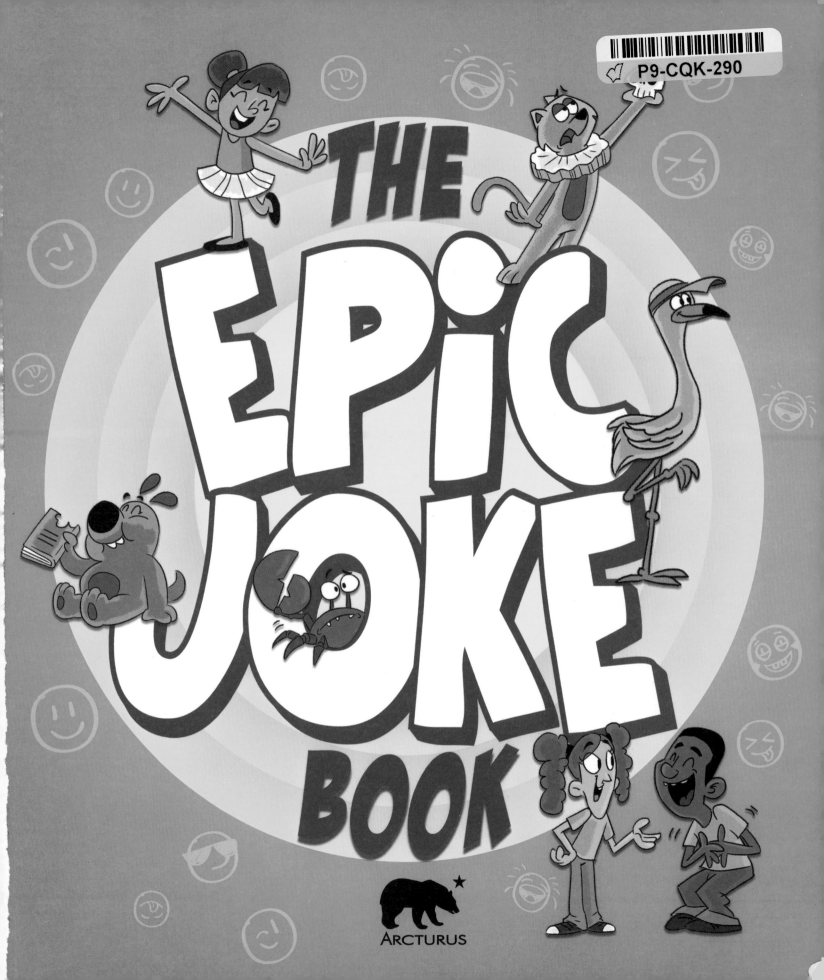

THE EPIC JOKE BOOK

ARCTURUS

This edition published in 2019 by Arcturus Publishing Limited
26/27 Bickels Yard, 151–153 Bermondsey Street,
London SE1 3HA

Author: Joe King
Illustrator: Leo Trinidad
Designer: Trudi Webb
With thanks to Tyler Scott

ISBN: 978-1-78950-610-5
CH007210NT
Supplier 29, Date 0919, Print run 8752

Printed in China

CONTENTS

5

What did the aquatic mammal say when it left the party?
"I'm otter here."
Why did the sickly crab walk sideways?
Its medicine had side effects!
Why is there no point playing jokes on snakes?
You can't pull their legs!

17

23

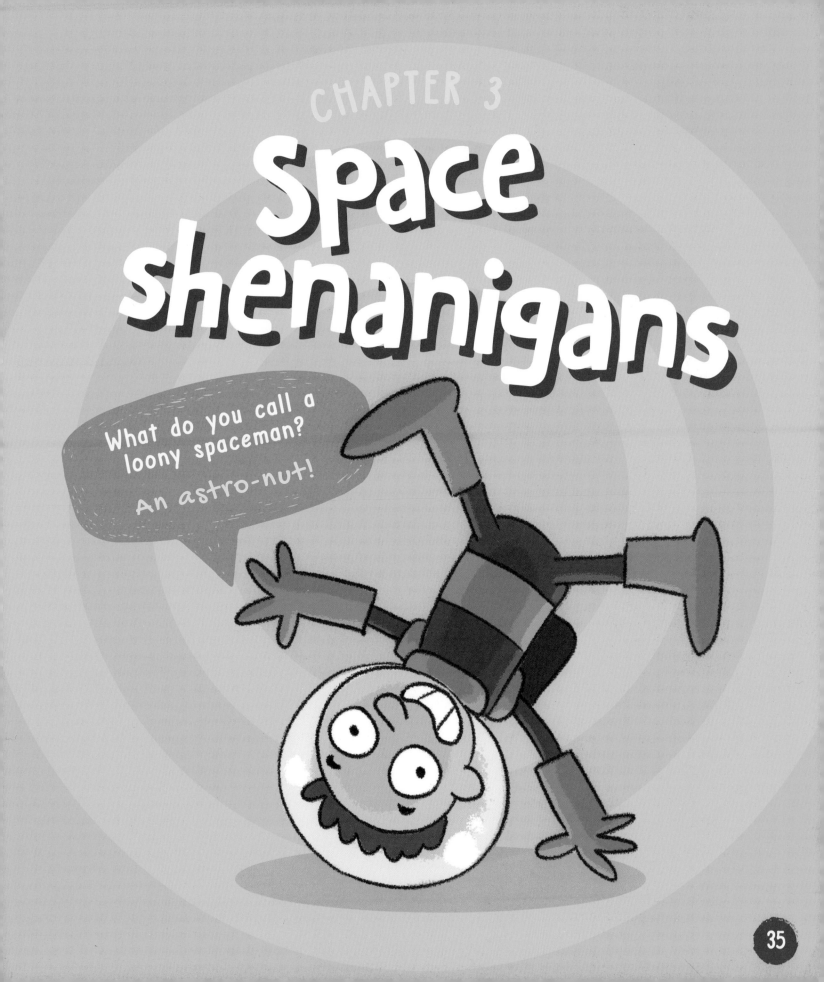

Why couldn't the planet find its way home?
Because it didn't know the Milky Way!
What kind of music do astronauts like?
Rocket 'n' roll!
What do you call a droid that goes the long way home?
R2-detour!

39

What do you call a sheep in space?
A ewe F. O.
How do you tie your shoes in space?
With astro-knots!
What did one shooting star say to the other shooting star?
"Pleased to meteor!"

44

45

What's the difference between a rocket and a fly?

A rocket can fly, but a fly can't rocket!

Why is the moon up so late these days?

Don't worry, he's just going through a phase!

What's the most dangerous thing in space?

A shooting star!

CHAPTER 4

Farmyard funnies
and
Preposterous pets

Which pets are the noisiest?
Trumpets!

51

Why did the scarecrow receive the Nobel prize?
Because he was out standing in his field!
What do you call a sleepy bull?
A bulldozer!
What's long, brown, and runs around a field?
A fence!

55

57

63

75

When do you go at red and stop at green?
When you're eating a watermelon!
What do you call a green vegetable that breaks out of prison?
An escapea!
Why can you never go hungry at the beach?
Because of all the sand which is there!

CHAPTER 6

Ye olde jests and japes

Why were the early days of history called the Dark Ages?

Because there were so many knights!

Which emperor should have stayed away from gunpowder?

Napoleon Blownapart!

Why were the ancient Egyptians good at spying?

They kept things under wraps!

Why did the pirate give his ship a coat of paint?

Because its timbers were shivering!

85